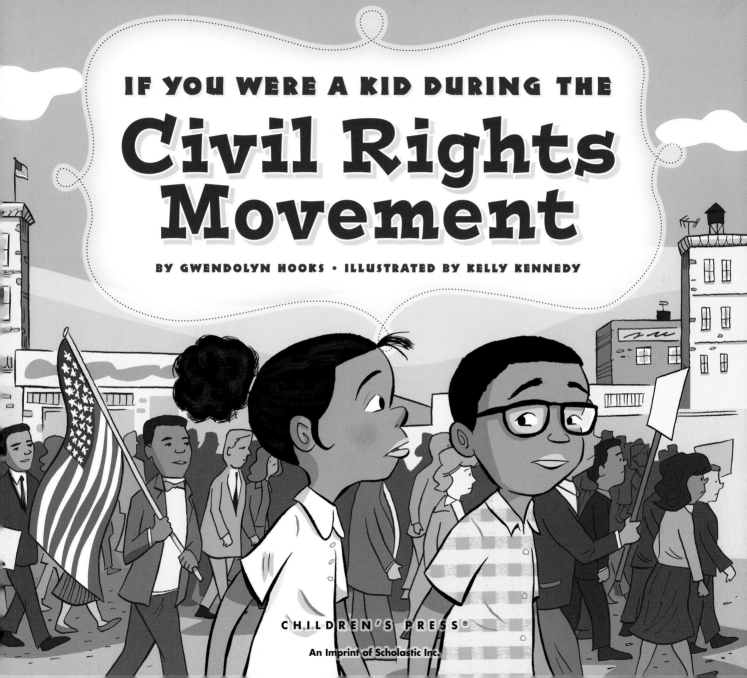

IF YOU WERE A KID DURING THE
Civil Rights
Movement

BY GWENDOLYN HOOKS • ILLUSTRATED BY KELLY KENNEDY

CHILDREN'S PRESS®

An Imprint of Scholastic Inc.

Content Consultant
James Marten, PhD, Professor and Chair, History Department, Marquette University, Milwaukee, Wisconsin

NOTE TO THE READER, PARENT, LIBRARIAN, AND TEACHER: This book combines a historical fiction narrative with nonfiction fact boxes. While all the nonfiction fact boxes are historically accurate and true, the fiction comes solely from the imaginations of the author and illustrator.

Photos ©: 9: AP Images; 11: Schomburg Center for Research in Black Culture, Jean Blackwell Hutson Research and Reference Division/New York Public Library; 13: Bettmann/Getty Images; 15: Underwood Archives/ Getty Images; 17: Bettmann/Getty Images; 19: AP Images; 21: Wally McNamee/Corbis/Getty Images; 23: Bettmann/Getty Images; 25: Christian Herb/Getty Images; 27: Philip Gould/Getty Images.

Library of Congress Cataloging-in-Publication Data
Names: Hooks, Gwendolyn, author. | Kennedy, Kelly (Illustrator), illustrator.
Title: If you were a kid during the civil rights movement / by Gwendolyn Hooks ; illustrated by Kelly Kennedy.
Description: New York : Children's Press, an imprint of Scholastic Inc.,
[2017] | Includes bibliographical references and index.
Identifiers: LCCN 2016038594| ISBN 9780531223840 (library binding) | ISBN 9780531230985 (pbk.)
Subjects: LCSH: African Americans—Civil rights—History—20th century—Juvenile literature. | Civil rights movements—United States—History—20th century—Juvenile literature. | Children—Southern States—History— 18th century—Juvenile literature. | United States—Race relations—Juvenile literature.
Classification: LCC E185.61 .H78 2017 | DDC 323.1196/073—dc23
LC record available at https://lccn.loc.gov/2016038594

TABLE OF CONTENTS

A Different Way of Life

The Civil War (1861–1865) freed African Americans from slavery. But even in the 1960s, a century later, they were not treated as equal citizens. They did not have **civil rights**. Laws in the southern states kept black and white Americans apart, or **segregated**. Imagine being an African American kid at this time. You would attend a different school than white kids. Your school would be in poor condition. You wouldn't be allowed to eat in restaurants that were only for whites. Instead, you would order your meals at the back door. On buses, you would have to sit in the back seats. Segregation was allowed under the law, and things were supposed to be "separate but equal" for white and black people. But though life was separate, it was not equal. African Americans were determined to be **integrated** into society and gain equal rights.

Meet Connie!

This is Connie Underwood. She lives with her parents and her older twin brothers, Robbie and Tommie, in Oklahoma. She and the twins have always been very close. She loves to climb her favorite tree to read and think up in its branches. Now she really has some thinking to do. The twins have a secret. Maybe that new boy who moved into the house behind hers can help solve this mystery. . . .

Meet Mark!

This is Mark Jenkins. His family used to live on an air force base in Washington, D.C. Now he has to get used to a new school in Oklahoma. His old school was integrated. That meant African American kids and white kids were in the same class. But his new school is segregated. Every kid is African American. School starts soon, and Mark wants to make a friend before then. It's not easy being the new kid. . . .

It was a hot August evening in 1963. Connie grabbed a soda and headed outside. She climbed her favorite tree and hid in its shade. Her brothers' voices floated into the backyard. She heard them use words like "sit-ins," "marches," and "civil rights." Connie did not understand what it all meant. Her brothers were up to something. But what?

EQUAL RIGHTS FOR ALL

Amendments to the U.S. Constitution guarantee certain rights. The end of slavery, protection from danger, and the right to vote are some of them. But many African Americans did not have these rights in the 20th century. The National Association for the Advancement of Colored People (NAACP) was formed in 1909. This organization works to protect the rights of African Americans and make sure they are treated equally.

Young men head to a sit-in in Oklahoma City in August 1960. Sit-ins were often organized by the NAACP.

Mark sat on the porch of his family's new home with two books. He was flipping back and forth between a mystery novel and *The Green Book*. Mark had started reading *The Green Book* during the long drive from Washington. His dad said they would have starved in the South without it. As he read, Mark thought about the friends he had left behind.

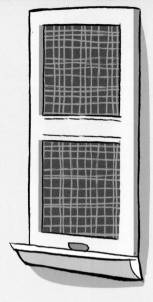

THE GREEN BOOK

African Americans traveling in the United States used *The Green Book* to plan their trips. This book was published from 1936 to 1964. It listed hotels, gas stations, and restaurants that welcomed African Americans. The book was very important to these travelers before the civil rights movement brought change.

A New York post office worker named Victor H. Green wrote *The Green Book*.

Connie spotted her new neighbor.
She climbed the fence into his backyard.
They introduced themselves, and Mark told
Connie about his move from Washington.

Connie looked at her new friend's
books. "I see you like mysteries," she said.

"I sure do!" Mark answered.

"Maybe tomorrow you can help
me solve one," Connie said. Then
she explained what had been
going on with her brothers.

"I HAVE A DREAM"

Dr. Martin Luther King Jr. was one of the most well-known civil rights leaders. He was famous for leading peaceful protests. In 1963, thousands of people attended his March on Washington to support civil rights. King gave a speech at the end of the march. In it, he said, "I have a dream that one day . . . little black boys and black girls will be able to join hands with little white boys and white girls as sisters and brothers."

When Dr. King spoke, his words moved people to action.

That night, Connie heard the twins talking in the backyard.

"It's on for tomorrow morning," Robbie said. "We meet downtown in front of Joey's Ice Cream at 10 o'clock."

"They'll think twice about not serving us," Tommie said.

Connie's heart thudded. Her brothers were planning to **demonstrate**! She had heard that demonstrators often got hurt. Some were sent to jail.

14

WOULD YOU GIVE UP YOUR SEAT?

In 1955, Rosa Parks boarded a bus in Montgomery, Alabama. As the bus filled, the driver ordered Mrs. Parks to give up her seat to a white man. She refused and was arrested. African Americans **boycotted** the city's buses in protest. They walked, used cabs, or carpooled instead. After 381 days, the city of Montgomery agreed to let African Americans sit where they wanted on buses.

Rosa Parks sits on a bus after the boycott.

The next morning, Mark watched Connie climb over the fence. "We have to hurry," Connie said. "I think the twins planned a civil rights demonstration downtown. I want to make sure they are okay."

Mark hesitated. He was afraid, but he wanted to help his new friend.

NINE BRAVE KIDS IN LITTLE ROCK

In September 1957, nine African American students volunteered to attend an all-white high school in Little Rock, Arkansas. The state's governor refused to let them enter. President Dwight Eisenhower sent federal troops to guard them on the way in and out of school. These brave students are known as the Little Rock Nine.

The Little Rock Nine are escorted by soldiers at the end of a school day.

Connie and Mark ran downtown. African American teenagers were marching on Main Street. Rows of marchers shouted, "Separate is not equal!" They filled the street like the town's high school band did before a big football game. Only these teens were not smiling. Connie and Mark squeezed through the marchers and looked for the twins.

A FIRST GRADER MAKES HISTORY

In 1960, first-grader Ruby Bridges became the first student to integrate schools in New Orleans, Louisiana. The U.S. Supreme Court had already ordered all schools to integrate. But most refused. Ruby's parents enrolled her in a white school. White parents didn't let their children attend class with Ruby. She had a teacher all to herself. Neither Ruby nor her teacher missed a day of school!

Ruby Bridges is escorted by U.S. Marshals to protect her from protesters.

FREEDOM NOW

White people with angry faces watched the demonstrators. Some shouted ugly words. Connie remembered her parents talking about the African Americans who rode in the front seats of buses from Alabama to Mississippi. They were hurt badly by angry white people. Could that happen to the twins?

Suddenly, someone shouted, "Police!" Connie knew the police sometimes hurt demonstrators. She grabbed Mark's hand.

POLICE VIOLENCE

The civil rights movement angered many white people. They did not want African Americans to be treated equally. Sometimes they became violent. African Americans could not rely on the police for protection. The police usually took the side of the **racist** white people.

Police attack a protester in Washington, D.C.

This was only Mark's second day in a new city. He'd never seen people so angry.

"We need help!" Mark hollered.

He and Connie squeezed to the back of the marchers as fast as they could. Then they sprinted to Connie's house. Mark's heart thudded with each step. He hoped Connie's mother would know what to do.

CHURCH BOMBED!

On September 15, 1963, members of a church in Birmingham, Alabama, were attending Sunday school classes. A bomb went off and killed four young girls. White men who were members of a violent racist group were to blame. The African American community was devastated. The explosion shocked the city.

Family members outside the funeral for one of the girls killed in the bombing

Connie quickly told her mother about the twins. Mrs. Underwood was angry, but not at the kids.

"Let's go get your brothers," she said. "They are trying to do the right thing, but they should have gotten a permit first! Then the police wouldn't be able to arrest them."

24

CIVIL RIGHTS ON TV

In the 1960s, many families bought televisions for the first time. They watched the evening news programs. They could see and hear exactly what was happening to protesters. More people learned about the civil rights movement. They would travel from all across the country to join demonstrations.

Viewers watched Martin Luther King Jr. and other civil rights leaders deliver stirring speeches on TV.

A few weeks later, Connie and Mark marched between the twins. Their parents were right behind them, carrying a parade permit. Now the police couldn't stop them. As they marched past Joey's Ice Cream, Connie looked at Mark and the twins. She knew they were all thinking the same thing. *One day, we'll walk right in the front door. We will order ice cream sodas. And we will twirl on those red-topped stools.*

EQUAL RIGHTS

THE CIVIL RIGHTS MEMORIAL

The Civil Rights Memorial in Montgomery, Alabama, honors people who died fighting for civil rights. On a stone wall, water flows across words from Dr. King's "I Have a Dream" speech. The words say that African Americans will not be satisfied "until justice rolls down like waters and righteousness like a mighty stream."

The names of 40 civil rights heroes are written on the memorial.

...UNTIL JUSTICE ROLLS DOWN LIKE WATERS AND RIGHTEOUSNESS LIKE A MIGHTY STREAM

MARTIN LUTHER KING JR

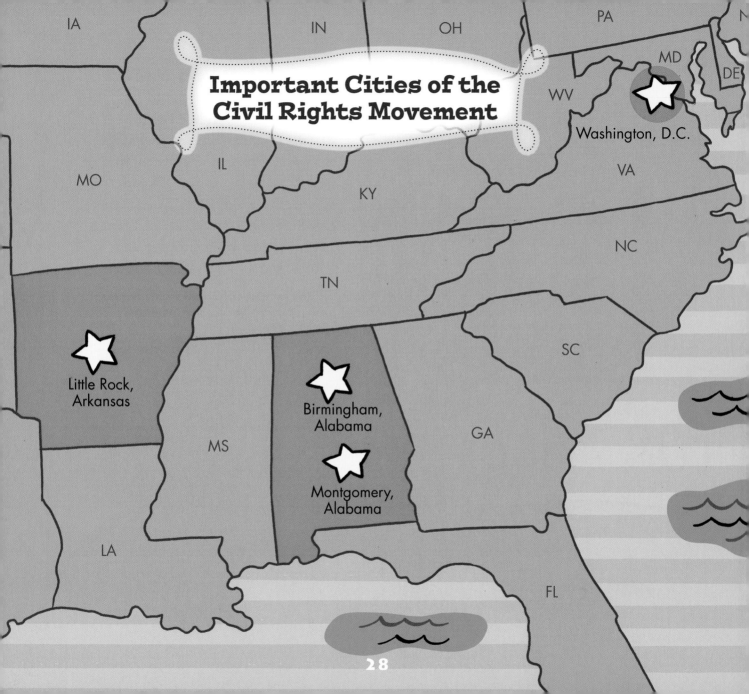

Important Cities of the Civil Rights Movement

IA

IN

OH

PA

MD

DE

MO

IL

WV

Washington, D.C.

VA

KY

NC

TN

SC

Little Rock,
Arkansas

Birmingham,
Alabama

GA

MS

Montgomery,
Alabama

LA

FL

Timeline

December 1955 Rosa Parks is ordered to give up her bus seat to a white passenger, which results in a bus boycott.

September 1957 The Little Rock Nine enroll in Little Rock Central High School. They are the first African Americans to attend an all-white school in Arkansas.

August 1963 Martin Luther King Jr.'s March on Washington is attended by thousands of people, both African American and white. Dr. King gives his famous "I Have a Dream" speech.

July 1964 The Civil Rights Act ends segregation in public places and in jobs. No longer can restaurants and hotels refuse to serve people. (It would take several more years before all the states followed the law.)

August 1965 The Voting Rights Act is passed to help protect voting rights of African Americans.

Words to Know

boycotted (BOI-kaht-id) refused to do business with someone as a punishment or protest

civil rights (SIV-uhl RITES) the individual rights that all members of a democratic society have to freedom and equal treatment under the law

demonstrate (DEM-uhn-strayt) to join together with other people to protest something

integrated (IN-tuh-grate-id) brought all races into equal membership in society

marches (MAR-chiz) large, organized groups of people walking together to protest or support something

racist (RAY-sist) practicing unfair or cruel treatment of people based on their race

segregated (SEG-ri-gay-tid) kept apart from the main group

sit-ins (SIT-inz) demonstrations where protesters would fill the seats of segregated restaurants so no one could eat there

Index

ABOUT THE AUTHOR

Gwendolyn Hooks lives in Oklahoma City, Oklahoma. She writes for young readers to encourage them to explore the world through books.

ABOUT THE ILLUSTRATOR

Born and raised in Los Angeles, California, Kelly Kennedy got his start in the animation business doing designs and storyboards at Nickelodeon. Since then, he's drawn and illustrated for a variety of children's books and magazines and is currently working on some of his own stories. When not drawing, he can be found working on his old cars or playing guitar in a bluegrass band.

Visit this Scholastic Web site for more information about the Civil Rights Movement:

www.factsfornow.scholastic.com
Enter the keywords **Civil Rights Movement**